Tell Me Why

WHY?

Chameleons Change Color

Katie Marsico

Published in the United States of America by Cherry Lake Publishing
Ann Arbor, Michigan
www.cherrylakepublishing.com

Content Adviser: Andrew M. Durso, PhD candidate at Utah State University
Reading Adviser: Marla Conn, ReadAbility, Inc

Photo Credits: © snowblurred/Shutterstock Images, 5; © Svoboda Pavel/Shutterstock Images, 7; © taboga/
Shutterstock Images, 9; © Arto Hakola/Shutterstock Images, 9; © belizar/Shutterstock Images, cover, 1, 9;
© Dennis van de Water/Shutterstock Images, 9; © Eric Isselee/Shutterstock Images, cover, 1, 11; © nevenm/
Shutterstock Images, 13; © Juan G. Aunion/Shutterstock Images, 15; © Amanda Winter/Shutterstock Images,
17; © Hugh Lansdown/Shutterstock Images, 19; © bikeriderlondon/Shutterstock Images, cover, 1, 21

Library of Congress Cataloging-in-Publication Data

Marsico, Katie, 1980- author.
  Chameleons change color / by Katie Marsico.
    pages cm.—(Tell me why?)
  Summary: "Young children are naturally curious about animals. Chameleons Change Color offers
answers to their most compelling questions about how chameleons camouflage themselves. Age-
appropriate explanations and appealing photos encourage readers to continue their quest for knowledge.
Additional text features and search tools, including a glossary and an index, help students locate
information and learn new words."—Provided by publisher.
  Audience: Ages 6–10
  Audience: K to grade 3
  Includes bibliographical references and index.
  ISBN 978-1-63362-609-6 (hardcover)—ISBN 978-1-63362-699-7 (pbk.)—
ISBN 978-1-63362-789-5 (pdf)—ISBN 978-1-63362-879-3 (ebook)
  1. Chameleons—Juvenile literature. 2. Camouflage (Biology)—Juvenile literature. 3. Adaptation
(Biology)—Juvenile literature. 4. Children's questions and answers. I. Title. II. Series: Tell me why?
(Cherry Lake Publishing)

QL666.L23M355 2016
597.95'6—dc23

                              2015005643

Cherry Lake Publishing would like to acknowledge the work of the Partnership for 21st Century Skills.
Please visit www.p21.org for more information.

Printed in the United States of America
Corporate Graphics

Table of Contents

Meet a Magical Lizard!

Nate is at an animal **sanctuary** on a school field trip. The class is listening to a volunteer talk about chameleons. But now it seems more like a magic show instead! The bright green lizard she is showing the students suddenly begins to turn dark brown.

The volunteer explains that this isn't unusual for chameleons. She says that some have the ability to change color. Nate is amazed. And he is a little curious about *why* chameleons do this.

Chameleons are known for being able to change the colors of their skin.

Chameleons are found in zoos, sanctuaries, and pet stores all over the world. In the wild, however, they mainly live in Africa, Asia, and southwestern Europe. Wild chameleons exist in a wide variety of **habitats**. These include rainforests, grasslands, and deserts.

A chameleon eats insects. But this **reptile** is a meal for many animals. Snakes and certain birds and mammals are some of the **predators** that eat chameleons.

This chameleon is using its tongue to catch an insect.

Most chameleons reach a length of between 0.9 and 23 inches (2.3 and 58.4 centimeters). They have a long tail and tongue, as well as a pair of large eyes. Their eyes are capable of looking in two separate directions at the same time!

Chameleons are perhaps most famous for their coloring. Sometimes the lizards show various shades of green, blue, turquoise, purple, black, and brown. In other cases, they are pink, red, orange, and yellow.

Look at these pictures of different chameleons. What colors do you see? Do you notice any patterns?

These are only a few of the many colors found in chameleons.

9

A Closer Look at Skin Layers

As Nate studies the chameleon, it starts to turn green again! He wonders aloud how it's possible for the lizard to do that. The volunteer says the answer involves the chameleon's four layers of skin.

The outer layer protects the layers underneath it. The next layer is filled with yellow and red **pigments**. The layer of skin beneath that contains darker pigments that create darker colors. Finally, the bottom layer only reflects shades of white.

Are you able to guess how many layers of skin people have? What color pigments do you think those layers contain?

A chameleon can change its skin color because of how its pigments are arranged.

A chameleon's **nerve** impulses, or signals, make the pigments grow and shrink. As the pigments grow and shrink, the different layers of a chameleon's skin blend together. The mixed pigments trigger color changes. These changes are often noticeable to observers such as Nate and his classmates.

This chameleon might change to another color when its surroundings change.

Reasons for Shifting Shades

The chameleon's ability to change color impresses Nate. But he still isn't sure why they shift shades. He guesses that the answer involves **camouflage**.

To Nate's surprise, the volunteer says that chameleons don't have to blend in with their surroundings to stay safe. They rely on their ability to move quickly to escape predators. The volunteer says that one of the main reasons chameleons change color is to communicate.

Chameleons use color to camouflage themselves,
but they have other ways to stay safe too.

Scientists believe that different colors send certain signals to other chameleons. Chameleons probably turn lighter shades in order to attract **mates**. It's possible that the darker shades are used to show anger.

Scientists also think that chameleons switch colors to adjust to their physical surroundings. It's their bodies' way of reacting to changes in temperature, light, and **humidity**. For instance, darker shades absorb, or soak up, more heat than lighter colors. So, if the outside temperature drops, chameleons stay warm by turning darker.

Want to know more about what color changes in chameleons mean? Ask a herpetologist! That's a scientist who studies reptiles.

This chameleon could be trying to send a message to other chameleons by the colors of its tail.

Chameleon Conservation

Nate decides he wants to learn more about chameleons. It turns out that many scientists feel the same way. But the volunteer says this will be difficult if people don't take more steps toward **conservation**.

She explains that chameleons face several threats. The largest involves their habitat being destroyed. When people clear forests for wood or to develop land, wildlife often suffers.

Rainforests, like this one in Madagascar, are a main habitat of chameleons.

The pet trade also affect chameleons. They don't always do well in **captivity**. In some cases, owners don't know how to properly care for their pets.

The volunteer tells Nate's class how to help chameleons. An important step is raising awareness about these remarkable reptiles. Nate is eager to do his part to protect chameleons. In the meantime, he has one final question for the volunteer. What color will the chameleon at the sanctuary turn next?

Chameleons are popular pets. But they don't always live in captivity as long as they do in the wild.

Think About It!

Go online to find out which other animals can change color. Think about how, when, and why the animals you have listed turn different colors.

Does your skin ever change color? What do you think causes these changes? Are the reasons similar to or different from what causes chameleons to change color?

Glossary

camouflage (KAM-uh-flahzh) natural coloring that allows animals to hide by making them look like their surroundings

captivity (kap-TIV-i-tee) the condition of being held or trapped by people

conservation (kahn-sur-VAY-shuhn) the act of working to protect an environment and the wildlife within it

habitats (HAB-ih-tatz) places where plants and animals normally live and grow

humidity (hyoo-MID-ih-tee) the amount of moisture in the air

mates (MAYTS) animals that join with other animals to produce young

nerve (NURV) a body part that controls movement and feeling by carrying messages between the brain and other parts of the body

pigments (PIG-muhntz) natural substances that give color to plants and animals

predators (PREH-duh-turz) animals that kill and eat other animals as food

reptile (REP-tile) a cold-blooded animal with a backbone and scales that breathes air and reproduces on land; most reptiles have four legs and reproduce by laying eggs

sanctuary (SANGK-choo-er-ee) a place where animals are given shelter and protection from any threats they face

Find Out More

Books:

Gish, Melissa. *Chameleons*. Mankato, MN: Creative Paperbacks, 2014.

Hansen, Grace. *Chameleons*. Minneapolis: ABDO Kids, 2015.

Murray, Peter. *Chameleons*. Mankato, MN: The Child's World, 2015.

Web Sites:

National Wildlife Federation—Chameleons
www.nwf.org/Kids/Ranger-Rick/Animals/Amphibians-and-Reptiles/Chameleons.aspx
Learn more about chameleons and conservation efforts.

Wonderopolis—Why Do Chameleons Change Their Colors?
http://wonderopolis.org/wonder/why-do-chameleons-change-their-colors/
Find out more about how and why certain chameleons shift from one color to another.

Index

About the Author

Katie Marsico is the author of more than 200 children's books. She lives in a suburb of Chicago, Illinois, with her husband and children.